THE DIAMOND CAPITAL

Yellowknife

JANICE PARKER

Published by Weigl Educational Publishers Limited
6325 – 10 Street SE
Calgary, Alberta, Canada
T2H 2Z9
Web site: http://www.weigl.com

National Library of Canada Cataloguing in Publication Data
Parker, Janice.
 Yellowknife

   (Canadian Cities)
   Includes Index
   ISBN 1-896990-73-8

   1. Yellowknife (N.W.T)--Juvenile literature. I. Title. II. Series:
Canadian Cities (Calgary, Alta)
FC4196.33.P37 2001   j971.9'3   C2001-910653-X
F1100.5.Y4P37 2001

Printed and bound in Canada
1 2 3 4 5 6 7 8 9 0   05 04 03 02 01

Project Coordinator
Jill Foran
Design
Warren Clark
Cover Design
Terry Paulhus
Layout
Lucinda Cage
Photo Researcher
Tina Schwartzenberger

We acknowledge the
financial support of
the Government of
Canada through the
Book Publishing
Industry Development
Program (BPIDP) for
our publishing activities.

Photograph Credits
Every reasonable effort has been made to trace ownership and to obtain permission to reprint copyright material.
The publishers would be pleased to have any errors or omissions brought to their attention so that they may be
corrected in subsequent printings.

Cover: Tessa Macintosh; Inside cover: Lyn Hancock; Corbis: page 18B; Corel: page 27T; Courtesy Northwest
Territories Arctic Tourism: pages 14T, 27B; Ekati Diamond Mine: pages 5B, 30BL; Lyn Hancock: pages 5M, 8T,
11T, 12M, 12BR, 13T, 13B, 14B, 15B, 16T, 16B, 17T, 17B, 19, 20B, 21T, 22T, 22B, 23L, 24T, 24B, 26B, 28T,
28B, 29B; Tessa Macintosh: pages 3R, 3B, 4R, 10B, 12BL, 15T, 18T, 20T, 21B, 23R, 25T, 25B, 26T, 29T;
National Archives of Canada: pages 6T (C2146), 10T (C060469); Northwest Territories Archives: pages 7T
(N-1979-052-3833), 8B (N-1990-003-0161), 9T (N-1994-004-0010), 9M (N-1987-033-0221), 9B (N-1979-052-3957),
30BR (N-1979-052-3957); Photofest: page 11B; Travel Montana/S. Shimek: pages 3L, 7B; www.canadianheritage.org
ID #10189, National Archives of Canada C20053: page 6B.

Contents

Introduction

Yellowknife is the capital city of the Northwest Territories. It is located on the west shore of Yellowknife Bay, which lies on the north arm of Great Slave Lake. Yellowknife is the only community in the Northwest Territories with a population over 5,000.

Yellowknife

Canada
0   500 km

Getting There

The easiest way to reach Yellowknife is by airplane. The city's airport hosts daily flights to and from Edmonton and Winnipeg and also offers flights to other communities in the North. People who wish to drive to Yellowknife can reach the city via the Mackenzie Highway.

At a Glance

Climate

Yellowknife's climate goes from one extreme to the other. Temperatures can range from 30° Celsius in the summer to –56°C in the winter. Summers are generally short and sunny, with an average high temperature of 21°C in July. Winters are cold, with lots of snow, and an average low temperature of –29°C in January. Winters in Yellowknife are darker than they are in most other capital cities. This is because the city lies only 512 km south of the **Arctic Circle**. On the shortest day of the year, usually December 21, Yellowknife receives just over four hours of sunlight. In the summer, however, the city enjoys very long hours of sunlight. At the height of summer, the sun is still up at midnight!

Area & Population

Yellowknife covers an area of 102 square kilometres and is made up of two sections—Old Town and New Town. Old Town is the city's original town site, located on Latham Island. It is connected to the mainland—New Town—by a bridge. The newer part of the city was built in the late 1940s, when the area underwent a mining **boom**. Today, over 17,500 people live in Yellowknife.

A Sparkling Future

Yellowknife calls itself the "Diamond Capital of North America." In October 1998, North America's very first diamond mine began operation in Yellowknife. The Ekati Diamond Mine is located about 300 km northeast of the city, and about 260 of the mine's employees live in Yellowknife. In 1999, Sirius Diamond Limited opened a diamond plant for cutting and polishing diamonds. Many Yellowknife residents work in diamond-related industries. More diamond mines and production plants are scheduled to open in the coming years. The diamond industry has become a central part of the economy in the Yellowknife region.

Interesting Statistics

1. About 90 percent of all air travel to and from the Northwest Territories is based out of Yellowknife Airport.

2. Yellowknife is the only city in the Northwest Territories. The territory also has four towns, one village, ten hamlets, three settlements, and four charter communities.

3. More than 25 percent of the population of the Northwest Territories lives in Yellowknife.

4. Yellowknife is the second most northerly capital city in Canada. Iqaluit, Nunavut, is the first.

5. The Great Slave Lake is the fifth largest freshwater lake in North America. The lake covers 28,568 sq km.

The Past

Alexander MacKenzie was born in Scotland. He returned there after 1808.

Early Settlement

People have lived in the Yellowknife area for thousands of years. Among the earliest occupants were the Dogrib, an Athapaskan-speaking group who hunted caribou. European explorers began to arrive in the region in the eighteenth century. In 1786, Peter Pond, an employee of a fur-trading company called the North West Company, established Fort Providence near the mouth of Yellowknife Bay. Three years later, explorer Alexander Mackenzie arrived in the area and operated Fort Providence as a trading post. During that time, the Yellowknife band of the Chipewyan nation moved into the area to take part in the fur-trading industry. The Yellowknife got their name from their knives, which were made of yellow-coloured copper blades. Soon enough, the bay, and then the community, were named after this band.

In the 1820s, Fort Providence closed, likely because better areas existed elsewhere for fur trading. Then, in 1896, prospectors travelling to the Klondike region of the Yukon discovered gold at Yellowknife Bay. The discovery brought few people to the remote region because the gold deposits were not large. However, in the 1930s, when air travel opened up the North and more gold-bearing deposits were discovered in Yellowknife Bay, many miners headed for the area. By 1937, three gold mines had been established, and the settlement continued to grow.

Key Events

1771 Samuel Hearne reaches Great Slave Lake.

1786 Fort Providence is established in the region.

1789 Alexander Mackenzie travels to the Yellowknife area and begins to operate Fort Providence as a trading post.

The Government

In 1939, the Yellowknife Administration District was created, and the first municipal government was in place. By 1940, about 1,000 people were living in the area. When further gold was found in the Giant Yellowknife Mine in 1946, more people moved to the region. The town was becoming overcrowded. This prompted the creation of a new town site. Construction of New Town, which would have sewer and water systems and **hydroelectricity**, began in 1947. Yellowknife became a Municipal District in 1953. At that time, the town elected its first mayor.

In 1967, Yellowknife was chosen to be the capital of the Northwest Territories. Three years later, it was incorporated as a city. Today, the territorial government continues to meet in Yellowknife. The municipal government has grown to include one mayor and eight councillors. The council oversees all of Yellowknife's municipal activities, including city planning and zoning, land developments, property taxes, fire protection, transportation, water and sewage, and recreation programs.

The construction of a hydroelectric station on Snare Lake in 1948 helped make New Town possible by providing power for the area.

1820 Explorer Sir John Franklin reaches the Coppermine River.
1896 Gold is discovered in the Yellowknife region.

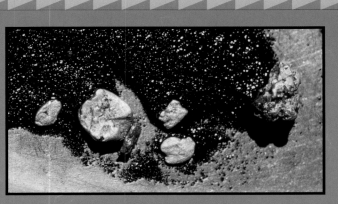

1920s Detachments of the RCMP keep law and order in the Northwest Territories.

Law and Order

During the early days of the Northwest Territories, there was little need for policing because the area's population was so small. As trading posts began to appear in the territory, disorder and lawbreaking became more of a threat. By the 1920s, **detachments** of the Royal Canadian Mounted Police (RCMP) could be found throughout the Canadian Arctic. Today, the RCMP "G" Division polices all of the Northwest Territories. Its headquarters are located in Yellowknife.

The city government also has its own policing division. The Municipal Enforcement Division enforces all the city's by-laws, which include highway traffic, noise control, and snowmobile and all-terrain vehicle by-laws.

Yellowknife RCMP officers work to maintain peace and order in the area. They patrol on boat, bicycle, and snowmobile.

By the 1920s, detachments of the Royal Canadian Mounted Police could be found throughout the Canadian Arctic.

Key Events

1930s More gold is discovered in the region, this time attracting miners and settlers.

1938 Yellowknife becomes a village.

1947 Construction of Yellowknife's New Town begins.

Early Transportation

In the past, getting to Yellowknife was difficult. There were no railways to the area, and driving took a very long time. In the winter months, driving was often impossible. Air travel was the mode of transportation that opened up the Canadian North. During the 1920s and 1930s, bush pilots flew from Edmonton and other major centres to northern regions carrying mail and supplies.

Early Native Peoples in Yellowknife travelled by snowshoe, kayak, or dogsled. Dogsleds were the fastest way to travel on snow or ice. In the 1940s, the Con Mine used dog teams to transport bars of gold to the Yellowknife Post Office.

World War II and Yellowknife

The events of World War II had a devastating effect on Yellowknife's growth. Throughout most of the 1930s, gold mining had drawn a number of settlers to the Yellowknife region. However, gold was not useful to outside markets during wartime. Gold production in the region slowed in the early 1940s and then stopped completely in 1944. Many gold miners left the area, and others were sent away to help in the war effort. Yellowknife's economy suffered. Once the war ended, the Giant Mine reopened, and a large amount of gold was discovered. This prompted another mining boom.

Dogsleds are still used as a method of transportation, and for sport, in the North.

1953 Yellowknife becomes a municipal district and elects its first mayor.

1967 Yellowknife is named capital of the Northwest Territories.

1970 Yellowknife is declared a city.

Famous People

Clennell Haggerston Dickins 1899–1995

Clennell Haggerston Dickins helped to open up the North. Clennell, nicknamed "Punch," was a pioneer bush pilot who flew great distances across the Northwest Territories. His skills as a pilot were highly respected. During World War I, he was awarded the Distinguished Flying Cross for gallantry in the Royal Flying Corps. In 1927, he joined Western Canadian Airways and soon began helping to establish communities in the Canadian North. In 1928 and 1929, Clennell flew the first prospectors into the Great Bear Lake area. His courage and skill as a bush pilot helped others to realize that the North could be reached by plane, and that settlement and development were possible.

Clennell Haggerston Dickins was named an Officer of the Order of Canada in 1968.

Nellie Cournoyea 1940–

Nellie Cournoyea grew up in the Northwest Territories with a traditional Inuvialiut lifestyle. In the 1960s she worked as a radio manager and announcer for CBC Radio. Nellie was elected to the Legislative Assembly of the Northwest Territories in 1979. When she was elected government leader of the Northwest Territories in 1991, she became the first Native woman to lead a provincial or territorial government in Canada. Nellie worked for the Northwest Territorial government for sixteen years.

Nellie Cournoyea helped negotiate the Nunavut Land Claims Agreement.

Max Ward
1921–

Max Ward was born in Edmonton. In 1940, he joined the Royal Canadian Air Force and served as a flight instructor during World War II. When the war ended, Max decided to work as a bush pilot. During his time as a bush pilot, he survived four plane crashes. In 1946, he organized Polaris Charter Company Limited, a transportation company that serviced northern destinations. The small company was based in Yellowknife and operated only one single-engined airplane. In 1953, Max bought a $100,000 bush plane and started Wardair Limited. This company was also based in Yellowknife, and it was the first to transport heavy equipment by air to northern regions. Wardair grew to include more aircraft, and was soon

One of Max Ward's airplanes is on display just outside the city.

offering transatlantic flights. In 1961, Max changed the company's name to Wardair Canada. It went on to become one of the biggest air charter companies in the country.

Margot Kidder
1948–

Actress Margot Kidder was born in Yellowknife. As a child, her family moved from place to place, and she had the opportunity to live in many different Canadian communities. Although she had no formal theatrical training while growing up,

Margot had a natural talent for acting. As a teenager, she performed in a number of Canadian television programs. Then, in 1969, Margot made her film debut in an American movie called *Gaily Gaily*. She acted in other movies during the 1970s before landing her breakthrough role as Lois Lane in *Superman*, one of the biggest movies of 1978. Margot also starred in the Superman sequels in the 1980s and has gone on to act in a number of television movies.

In addition to being an actress, Margot Kidder is an author and a spokesperson for mental health.

Charles Fipke and Stewart Blusson

Canadian geologist Charles Fipke had dreamed of finding diamonds since he was 17 years old. He began looking for them in the Northwest Territories in 1981. Early on in his search, he gained a knowledgeable partner named Stewart Blusson. Together, the two of them searched the cold, and often dangerous, lands of Canada's northwest regions. In 1990, they discovered diamond indicator materials near Lac de Gras, about 300 km northeast of Yellowknife. This discovery soon led to the biggest staking rush in Canadian history and the opening of Canada's first Diamond mine, Ekati.

Culture

Northern Arts

Yellowknife is the arts centre of the Northwest Territories. Yellowknife artists, such as Patricia Stacey, capture the spirit of the territory in their artwork. Many local stores in the city sell Dene craftwork and Inuit sculpture. In July, the Festival of the Midnight Sun focuses on local art and artisans. The festival features "Art in the Park," which introduces children

Baskets made of birchbark are among the many Dene crafts available in the city.

and adults to different types of artwork. Artist demonstrations and various workshops teach people how to paint, draw, or sculpt. There are also opportunities to learn the methods of traditional Native craft-making, including moose hair tufting and beading.

For those who are interested in live performances, the Northern Arts and Cultural Centre (NACC) has many shows throughout the year. The 313-seat theatre hosts a variety of musical and theatrical acts. Many local entertainers and musicians have performed in the theatre, along with a number of international acts.

FESTIVALS

After a long, cold winter, people in Yellowknife celebrate spring with the popular **Caribou Carnival** in March. The Canadian Championship Dog Derby is held during the Carnival, as are ice sculpting contests and snowmobile races. Some of the more unusual events are bannock and tea-making contests and the Ugly Truck and Dog Contest.

The Northern Arts and Cultural Centre was opened in 1984. It presents a variety of performances throughout the year.

Holidays Throughout the Year

Holidays in Yellowknife are celebrated with great energy. People in Yellowknife observe the same holidays as other Canadians. The city celebrates National Aboriginal Day in June. This day honours the history and culture of the country's Native Peoples. Canada Day in Yellowknife is celebrated with a parade, citizenship presentations, live music, food tasting, and activities such as face painting and racing. Labour Day weekend is celebrated with the Commissioner's Cup Race on Great Slave Lake. Sailboats in the race begin in Yellowknife, sail to Hay River, and then return to the city.

Every July 1, people in Yellowknife come together to celebrate Canada's birthday.

Yellowknifers celebrate the summer solstice with **Raven Mad Days**, a late-night festival for children and adults. Each year, Raven Mad Days features live music, sidewalk sales, games, and food from early evening until midnight. The **Under the Midnight**

Sun Festival is a three-day celebration of the performing arts in the city. It is held in July. The festival features plays, skits, dance performances, and storytelling. **Folk on the Rocks** is an annual folk music festival that attracts performers and visitors from all over the world.

In December, Yellowknife lights up with its Celebration of Lights. This celebration begins with the turning on of Christmas lights at City Hall and the Legislative Assembly. Many people also take part in the annual Christmas Light Contest. Prizes are given to the winners in five different categories, including best commercial exterior, commercial interior, residential exterior, neighbourhood exterior, and alternative lighting. On the last day of December—New Year's Eve—people in Yellowknife ring in the New Year with the First Night Celebration. This party features a bonfire, live entertainment, and fireworks.

Eating in Yellowknife

Yellowknife has many restaurants and cafés that serve everything from fast food, to traditional northern dishes, to dishes from around the world. Wild **game**, such as caribou and muskox, is served at many restaurants and is also eaten in many homes. Local fish, such as trout, whitefish, and arctic char, are other popular choices in Yellowknife. Another widely eaten food is bannock, a traditional bread in

Fishing in the Yellowknife area is popular among residents and tourists.

the Canadian North. Bannock is easy to make and can even be cooked in a frying pan over an open fire. Many people enjoy eating bannock with jam or jelly made from wild berries.

Groceries in Yellowknife can be more expensive than in other Canadian cities because it costs more to transport goods to the North. Prices can be especially high in the winter, when transportation is more difficult.

Caribou, muskox, and buffalo meat are usually sold in Yellowknife's grocery stores.

Bannock

1 l (4 cups) flour	
20 ml (4tsp) baking powder	
10 ml (2tsp) salt	
20 ml (4 tsp) sugar	
250 ml (1 cup) shortening	
175 ml (3/4 cup) raisins or currants	
500 ml (2 cups) milk	

Heat the oven to 230°C (450 °Fahrenheit). Combine the flour, baking powder, salt and sugar. Cut the shortening into the dry mixture until it resembles tiny pebbles. Add raisins if desired. Stir in milk. Roll out on a floured board to about a one-centimetre thickness and cut into round shapes. Bake for 15 minutes or until golden brown.

Cultural Groups in Yellowknife

Native Peoples make up about 25 percent of the city's residents. Among these peoples are the Dene, Métis, and Inuit. The Dene are the largest Native group in Yellowknife. There were once many different Dene groups, including the Dogrib and the Chipewyan. Traditionally, the Dene travelled around the northern regions to hunt for caribou, moose, and other animals. Today, the Dene living in the Yellowknife region are mainly descendants of the Dogrib.

The Métis in the Northwest Territories are descendants of the Dene and European fur traders who first visited the region. Today, about 7 percent of Yellowknife's residents are Métis. The Métis Nation is an organization that represents the interests of Métis people in the

The Dene celebrate their culture in many ways. These Dene are playing hand games outside the Prince of Wales Heritage Centre.

territory. Its head office is in Yellowknife. The North Slave Métis Alliance, also in Yellowknife, helps to promote Métis heritage and works to settle land claims. Only about 3 percent of Yellowknife's population is Inuit. Most Inuit live further east, in Canada's newest territory—Nunavut. The Inuit who live in the western Canadian Arctic call themselves Inuvialuit, or "the real people."

> **Native Peoples make up about 25 percent of the city's residents.**

A Varied Population

There are a number of cultural groups represented in Yellowknife. People with many different backgrounds have come from all over Canada and other parts of the world to live in the city. Many people moved to Yellowknife to work in the mining industry, while others moved there in search of a more peaceful lifestyle.

The Economy

The Centre of Things

Yellowknife is the industrial and economic centre of the Northwest Territories. Much of the territory's mining industry is based in the city. Gold was once the primary metal mined in the Yellowknife region. However, falling gold prices and other factors made gold less profitable in the 1990s. When the Giant Yellowknife Gold Mine closed down in 1999, the city's Miramar Con Mine became the only gold mine in the Northwest Territories. Diamond mining has taken over as the primary mining industry in the territory, and many people in Yellowknife work in diamond-related industries.

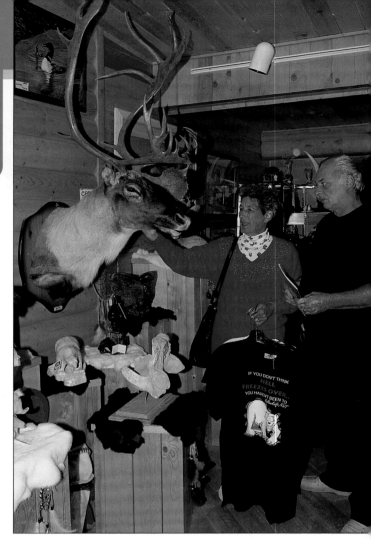

The Northwest Trading Post has a wide range of gift items for visitors who wish to take home souvenirs from Yellowknife.

The Ekati Diamond mine was officially opened on October 14, 1998. It employs about 650 people.

Yellowknife is also a centre for government. A significant number of people living in the city work for either the federal, territorial, or municipal government. These people are employed in the city's large service industry. Other people working in the service industry are employed as teachers, caretakers, tour guides, salespeople, or health care workers. The city is an important supply centre for other northern communities. People living in more remote communities often travel to Yellowknife to purchase supplies, visit a doctor, or watch a movie.

Travel and the Economy

The airline industry plays a large role in the city's economy.

Yellowknife is the centre of transportation for the Northwest Territories. Yellowknife Airport is one of the twenty busiest airports in Canada, operating over seventy flights per week. The city also has a reliable highway system and serves as an important destination point for people travelling to and from other northern communities.

Yellowknife is a popular destination for most visitors to the Northwest Territories. In fact, about 70 percent of the tourists who come to the territory visit the Yellowknife area. This makes tourism an important industry for the city. Most tourists visit Yellowknife in the warmer months, from May to August. However, in recent years, the winter months have brought many tourists to the region. This is because in the winter, Yellowknife is one of the best locations from which to view the **northern lights**. The city has a number of hotels, campgrounds, and tourist attractions to accommodate its visitors. Yellowknife's tourism industry is still growing, and many people in the city are working to develop this industry to its full potential.

Some of the more well-known guests of the Explorer Hotel have included Prime Minister Jean Chrétien, Queen Elizabeth, and Prince Philip.

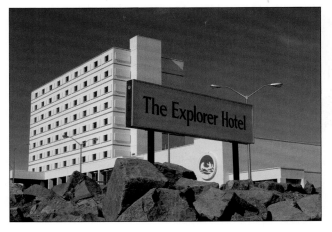

Getting Around in Yellowknife

Due to its small size, it is easy to walk from one place to another in Yellowknife. Many citizens use the scenic Frame Lake Trail to walk to work. This trail runs from Frame Lake south to downtown Yellowknife. Cycling is another popular way to get around the city, but only from April to October.

Almost all of the streets in Yellowknife are paved. Even during rush hour, it only takes a few minutes to drive across the city. Traffic is rarely a concern. The main concern Yellowknifers have with automobiles is ensuring that they will start during the cold winter months. The city also permits the use of snowmobiles in downtown streets.

Yellowknife has three bus routes that run on weekdays. Residents and visitors will often take taxis to get to their destinations. The city's small size means that taxi fares are usually inexpensive. Many Yellowknifers find taxis more convenient than starting and warming up their own vehicles in cold weather.

The Frame Lake Trail is 7 km long. About 4 km of the trail is paved.

Snowmobiling in the City

Many Yellowknifers use snowmobiles instead of cars to get around in the winter months. Just as people who drive cars must follow certain rules of the road, snowmobilers in Yellowknife have a set of rules they must obey. When driving on roads that are also used by cars, snowmobilers must keep as far to the right as possible, and yield the right of way to both pedestrians and cars. They must also obey all traffic signs, and observe the posted speed limit. When driving on city roads, snowmobilers may not exceed 45 km per hour, even in places where cars are permitted to go 70 km per hour.

Researching the North

Yellowknife has a number of excellent research facilities. The Yellowknife Public Library has more then 50,000 books, audiotapes, videos, and other materials that can be borrowed by library cardholders. The library reference collection contains a wealth of information on all kinds of topics.

People who wish to research the residents, culture, and history of the Canadian Arctic can visit the Prince of Wales Northern Heritage Centre. The centre has a research room that allows visitors to look at publications, reports, photographs, and other documents

The Prince of Wales Northern Heritage Centre is dedicated to preserving the culture and heritage of Dene, Métis, Inuit, and non-Native peoples of the Northwest Territories.

> *Yellowknife has a number of excellent research facilities.*

related to the Northwest Territories. It also offers educational tours and programs for local schools and visitors who want to learn more about the territory's heritage.

Some Yellowknife residents attend Aurora College. This college, which is based in Fort Smith, has a campus in Yellowknife. Students of the college can study programs such as management, education, or applied communications. The Aurora Research Institute, which is **affiliated** with the college, studies ways in which to improve and enrich life in the western part of the Northwest Territories.

Sports and Recreation

Northern Recreation

The Yellowknife area offers many opportunities for outdoor recreation. Hiking, boating, and fishing are just a few of the summer activities that draw people to the region. Yellowknife

also offers its residents and visitors tennis courts and a golf course. In June, the city hosts the Midnight Golf Tournament. This annual event is held on June 22. Players tee off at midnight, and, because the city is so close to the Arctic Circle,

Yellowknife's numerous lakes and rivers are popular with canoe enthusiasts.

the sun remains shining. Once summer has passed and winter arrives, many Yellowknifers enjoy snowmobiling, ice-fishing, and cross-country skiing. Yellowknife also has a number of indoor sporting facilities, including a swimming pool, a curling rink, two arenas, and a bowling alley.

The Yellowknife Golf Club has its own set of rules that golfers must follow.

Mushing for Sport

Yellowknife is home to the annual Canadian Championship Dog Derby. The race dates back to 1955, when the first dog-sled race was held in Yellowknife. The first race was about 64 km long, and the winner completed the race with his dog team in less than five and a half hours. He won $50. The other race winners won prizes such as rifle shells and groceries.

Today the race is over 240 km long and consists of three **heats**. The first prize winner is awarded $15,000.

The Canadian Championship Dog Derby is held in late March each year.

Racers must travel by a sled or toboggan pulled by ten dogs at the most. People from around the world come to compete in the race.

Yellowknife Sports Groups

Yellowknife is home to several local sports associations and leagues. The Yellowknife Badminton Club meets three evenings a week in a local school gymnasium. Many people in the city compete in broomball, a sport similar to hockey. Broomball players wear sneakers instead of skates,

and hit a small ball with paddle-shaped sticks. The Yellowknife Polar Bear Swim Club teaches kids to swim both competitively and for fun. Many Yellowknifers play softball as part of the city's Slo-Pitch Association, and runners in the city compete in the Yellowknife Marathon, which is held every fall. The city is also home to a cross-country ski club.

Tourism

Looking at History

The Prince Of Wales Northern Heritage Centre is one of the most popular tourist attractions in Yellowknife. Located on the shore of Frame Lake, this centre offers an exciting look into the history and culture of the Canadian North. It has excellent research and information facilities—including the Northwest Territories Archives—for visitors who wish to explore the documented history of the territory. It is also home to a museum that houses many exhibits related to northern culture and heritage. The centre's permanent collection contains about 100,000 artifacts, representing the archaeology, geology, plants, animals, and social history of the territory. Some exhibits depict aspects of Dene and Inuit culture. Others display fine collections of Inuit and Dene art. A giant stuffed polar bear and a moose-skin boat are also on display.

Among the centre's exhibits is a caribou-skin tent that dates back to the nineteenth century.

One gallery at the centre is devoted entirely to northern aviation. One of the earliest planes used in the North—the Fox Moth—is showcased in the gallery.

The Prince of Wales Northern Heritage Centre is a great place to learn more about the Northwest Territories. Along with the many exhibits, the centre offers slide presentations, performances, and lifelike **dioramas** that depict important historical events and even some of the regular activities of northern Canadians.

A moose-skin boat like the ones used by early Dene settlers is on display at the centre.

Trails of Fun

The Ingraham Trail is perfect for tourists who enjoy the outdoors. The trail starts near Yellowknife and winds for 70 km east of the city. Visitors who follow this trail gain access to other hiking trails, wilderness parks, campgrounds, picnic spots, and lakes, many of which have boat launches. Anglers may fish in several of the lakes along the trail, or they can hike to some of the more remote, often unnamed lakes. Hikers can choose from five hiking trails. Three campgrounds

The Ingraham Trail is perfect for tourists who enjoy the outdoors.

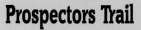

Prospectors Trail

Another interesting trail in Yellowknife is called Prospector's Trail. Located in Fred Henne Park, Prospector's Trail is an interpretive trail among gold-bearing rocks. Hikers along the 4-km loop have the opportunity to observe the region's varied ecological features. Signs along the trail tell the story of the area's rich geology.

along the trail are open from the middle of May to the middle of September.

The Ingraham Trail is a wonderful place for tourists who enjoy watching wildlife. Ospreys and eagles are often seen in the area. In the spring, peregrine falcons and flocks of tundra swans are also sighted. Barren ground caribou migrate through the area, and smaller animals such as wolves, hares, foxes, and beavers may be seen as well.

Each of the hiking paths along the Ingraham Trail offers fascinating scenery.

Old Town

Old Town sits on a narrow
peninsula that juts into Great
Slave Lake. This colourful area
was the original town site of
Yellowknife, and remains a
fun and vital part of the
city—especially for tourists.
Old Town still has many of its
old **frontier** buildings, most of
which have been preserved.
Visitors enjoy walking around
the historic area and discovering
the cottages and cabins that
were part of the city's early
days. Old Town also serves as
the base for several bush-pilot

*Many of Old Town's frontier buildings delight
tourists with their bright colours and
interesting decorations.*

operations, and visitors to the area
can take **floatplane** trips into the
surrounding countryside.

Bush pilots played a major role
in the development of Yellowknife
and the rest of the Northwest
Territories. With the help of early
bush pilots, the territory became
more accessible to settlers and
explorers. Many bush pilots
carried mail, medicine, and other
supplies into remote areas. The
Bush Pilot's Memorial is situated
in Old Town. This stone pillar
pays tribute to the pilots
who opened up the North.

*The Bush Pilot's Memorial
stands at the top of a hill
in Old Town.*

Light Show

Many tourists come to Yellowknife just to get a good view of the northern lights. During the winter months, this light show is easily seen from the city. In fact, the Yellowknife area is considered one of the best places to see the northern lights, also called the *aurora borealis*. Visitors from all over the world travel to the city to observe the stunning occurrence. The lights are created when solar winds thrust particles from the sun into Earth's atmosphere. When the lights rise, they look like flowing curtains in shades of red, lavender, and green. The northern lights ripple and stretch across the sky, creating an amazing scene.

Many companies in Yellowknife offer special tours for visitors wishing to see the northern lights.

Nahanni National Park Reserve

One of Canada's most beautiful National Parks is located within a 600-km drive of Yellowknife. Nahanni National Park Reserve is near Fort Simpson, in the southwest corner of the territory. Many visitors to Yellowknife travel to Nahanni National Park via floatplane. The park covers 4,766 sq km and contains some of the most beautiful scenery in North America. The region has a very diverse landscape: mountains, plains, wetlands, and forests are all a part of the park. The park is also home to the deepest river canyon in Canada, and a waterfall twice the height of Niagara Falls. The South Nahanni River's canyon is up to 1,200 metres deep, and Virginia Falls is about 90 m tall. Visitors to the park enjoy such activities as camping, white-water rafting, kayaking, and hiking. The Nahanni National Park Reserve is a UNESCO World Heritage Sight.

Architecture

The members of the Legislative Assembly meet in the circular Chamber and Public Gallery.

A Home for the Territorial Government

In 1993, the Legislative Assembly building of the Northwest Territories was completed, giving the territorial government its first permanent home in over a century. Two architects from the territory, Ferguson Simek Clark and Pin Matthews, designed the building together with an architectural firm

The Legislative Assembly building is the first permanent home for the territorial government since the 1880s when the council sat in Regina.

in Vancouver. Stone from the Yellowknife area forms the foundations of the building. The outside walls are covered in panels of zinc that are coloured light green. The domed roof is covered in zinc, as well. Zinc was used because it is mined in the North and because it weathers well.

The circular shape of the domed roof represents the cultural heritage of the peoples of the region and the **consensus** structure of the territorial form of government.

The Legislative Assembly was built a short distance from downtown Yellowknife. The landscape around the building has been preserved so that animals can continue to make their homes there.

In the Image of Man

One of the most striking pieces of architecture in the Northwest Territories is the Inukshuk, a figure built entirely of blocks of stone laid upon each other. Inukshuk is an Inuit word meaning "in the image of man." The plural of Inukshuk is Inukshuit. These figures were built throughout the Arctic. They were created from large slabs of rock and made to look like people with outstretched arms. Inuit have built Inukshuit for thousands of years.

There may have been several purposes for the Inukshuk. Much of the land in the North has few natural features that can be used as landmarks for travellers. Inukshuit were used as markers or as highway signs for the people of the North. If an Inukshuk is located near water, its open leg will point to the best route through the water. An Inukshuk located inland might point towards a mountain pass. One arm of an Inukshuk is usually longer than the other. This arm points travellers in the direction they should head.

Today, Inukshuit are still used by many Inuit hunters to mark trails and good hunting locations.

The Wildcat Café

One of the most popular landmarks in Yellowknife is the Wildcat Café in Old Town. Willy Wiley and Smokey Stout built the café in 1937. For many years it was a popular gathering place for people in the city. Pilots, miners, and prospectors would gather in the café and trade their tales of the North. The Wildcat Café opened the first ice cream stand in Yellowknife and also became the first restaurant in the city to serve Chinese food.

The Wildcat Café is made of logs. Most buildings that were constructed in the early years of Yellowknife, when it was difficult to bring building materials into the region, were very similar to the café. On the inside of the building, the log walls and pole ceiling are exposed. The Wildcat Café was refurbished and reopened in 1978.

Fascinating Facts

May they rest in Peace

NORTH OF 60° MINING MEMORIAL

This monument is dedicated to the men and women who lost their lives in the mining industry in the Northwest Territories

1 The Dene name for Yellowknife is *Sombak'e*, which means "money place."

2 Many of the diamonds produced in the territory have tiny images of polar bears lasered onto them.

3 Many people in Yellowknife have died in mining accidents. A monument honouring these miners stands near the Legislative Assembly building.

4 Yellowknife has one of the lowest unemployment rates in the country.

5 Some of the oldest rocks in the world have been found north of Yellowknife. These rocks have been dated at 4 billion years old.

6 The city crest, adopted in 1956, represents many of the city's features. It shows the mining industry, fishing, a yellow knife blade, the Great Slave Lake, the northern lights, the raven, and the midnight sun.

7 At least six different languages are spoken by residents of Yellowknife: Chipewyan, Dogrib, South and North Slavey, English, and French.

8 The Mackenzie Highway is the road that connects Yellowknife to Edmonton. Parts of this major highway are unpaved.

9 The Ekati Mine is now producing high-quality diamonds. The name "Ekati" is a Dogrib word meaning "fat lake." The name was given because the white quartz found there looked like caribou fat.

10 The Stanton Yellowknife Hospital serves the entire western Arctic.

Activities

Based on what you have read, try to answer the following questions.

Short Answer

 1 How many cities are there in the Northwest Territories?

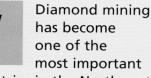 Diamond mining has become one of the most important industries in the Northwest Territories.

 2 Which is the largest group of Native Peoples in Yellowknife?

 3 What are the names of Yellowknife's two sections?

4 What tourist attraction draws many tourists to Yellowknife during the cold winter months?

5 Are traffic jams a big concern in downtown Yellowknife?

True or False

 6 The railway was responsible for bringing many settlers to the Yellowknife area.

7 Diamond mining has become one of the most important industries in the Northwest Territories.

8 Yellowknife is the most northerly capital city in Canada.

9 World War II had very little effect on Yellowknife because the city was so far away.

 10 Snowmobilers are allowed to drive on many of Yellowknife's streets.

Answers:
1. One. Yellowknife is the only city in the territory.
2. The Dene.
3. Old Town and New Town.
4. The northern lights.
5. No.
6. False. There are no railways connected to Yellowknife.
7. True. Many people in the city work in the diamond industry.
8. False. Iqaluit, Nunavut is more northern than Yellowknife.
9. False. World War II put a halt to Yellowknife's gold mining boom.
10. True. Snowmobilers have a set of rules they must obey when driving on the city's roads.

More Information

Books

Marshall, Diana. **Northwest Territories**. Calgary: Weigl Educational Publishers, 2001.

McDermott, Barb and Gail McKeown. **All About Capital Cities: Yellowknife**. Edmonton: Reidmore Books, 1999.

Schemenauer, Elma. **Hello Yellowknife**. Agincourt, Ontario: GLC Publishers Limited, 1986.

Web sites

City of Yellowknife homepage
http://city.yellowknife.nt.ca/

Northwest Territories government page
http://www.gov.nt.ca/

Prince of Wales Northern Heritage Centre
http://pwnhc.learnnet.nt.ca/splash.htm

Some Web sites stay current longer than others. To find information on Yellowknife, use your Internet search engine to look up such topics as "Ekati Diamond Mine," "Great Slave Lake," "The Canadian Championship Dog Derby," or any other topic you want to research.

Glossary

affiliated: officially connected to another organization

Arctic Circle: the line of latitude running through the northern hemisphere at about 66°33 North

boom: a period of growth and wealth

consensus: general agreement

detachments: groups of troops or ships sent out on special missions

dioramas: three-dimensional, lifelike scenes displaying figures, stuffed animals, and other objects against painted backgrounds

floatplane: an airplane with one or more floats used for landing on or taking off from water

frontier: land that forms the furthest extent of a country's inhabited or settled regions

game: wild animals hunted for food or sport

heats: different rounds in a race or contest

hydroelectricity: electricity produced by water power

northern lights: bands of light that appear in the northern sky at night

peninsula: a piece of land that is almost entirely surrounded by water

Index